THE RESOLVING CONFLICT POCKETBOOK

By Max A Eggert and Wendy Falzon

Drawings by Phil Hailstone

Dedication
For Kerry, whom we both love dearly and hope that all her conflicts will be minor.

CONTENTS

FROM THE AUTHORS

Daily life is full of the possibility, if not of overt conflict, then of disagreement, simply because there is not enough of what everyone wants to go around. Conflict and disagreements occur over money, goods, services, power, possessions and more. If something exists and more than one person wants or needs it, you have potential for conflict.

Conflict takes place at home and at work, between individuals, teams, groups, tribes, clans, nations and states. In fact, conflict is pretty ubiquitous. Where there are people there is usually conflict. Whether you are negotiating with your spouse or on behalf of your country, you have to learn the skills of empathy, listening and rapport, along with the ability to balance your emotional needs with your thinking. If you have power, coercion is easy, but it does not work in the long run.

Today the *win/lose* approach, risking a *lose/lose* outcome, is no way to resolve conflict. You might win the argument but lose the relationship. Win now, only to lose later.

Since conflict then is so endemic, perhaps even natural, it would be wise first to attempt to understand it and then consider ways to resolve it or use it positively. We hope that this book goes part way in assisting you in working through the inevitable conflict that you meet from time to time. Peace be with you.

HOW THIS BOOK WILL HELP YOU

Once you have worked through this book you should be able to:

- Understand what conflict is about
- Recognise the signs of conflict
- Understand how people react to conflict
- Develop strategies for dealing with conflict
- Understand conflict in organisation and work settings
- Have some ideas about how to resolve difficulties
- Have a better understanding of two important categories of conflict at work:
  - bullying
  - sexual harassment

WHAT IS CONFLICT?

WHAT IS CONFLICT?

DEFINITION

Conflict happens when two or more parties (point 1, below), one usually with more power (2), assert that they have a right to a limited resource or a course of action (3) and those involved in the situation can frustrate the desires of the other(s) (4).

Points to note:

1. Conflict can occur between more than two parties.

2. If one party has absolute power then there may be a need for conflict resolution but there is no negotiation. *Might becomes right* and what is wanted is just taken. Remember the old joke: 'Where does a 6-foot 6-inch, 20 stone man with a sub-machine gun sit in a packed underground carriage?'. Answer: 'Anywhere he pleases!'.

3. With an unlimited resource, such as the air we breathe, there would be no conflict. Usually if you put a price on something it can lead to conflict.

4. Each of the parties can counter or frustrate the requirement of the other(s). If they cannot then there will be no conflict, but point (2) above will still apply.

WHAT IS CONFLICT?

DEFINITION

The content, requirements or *fuels* for conflict are:

- Two or more parties wanting a limited resource
- A perceived legitimacy to that resource by the parties
- Interdependency of the parties - they need each other
- No gross differences in power

Note: It could be said that if one party had absolute power and took the disputed resource from the other party or parties, there would still be conflict, because those dominated would feel aggrieved. This would be so, but in such cases any conflict resolution methods, and certainly the ones outlined here, would not help. A subject cannot negotiate with a dictator; only another dictator can do that. Unfortunately, history has taught us that *might is right* (see page 16).

BENEFITS OF CONFLICT

- ✔ Conflict promotes growth, through learning to overcome challenges in unison with others
- ✔ It promotes creativity and innovation as solutions are suggested to overcome the differences between the stakeholders
- ✔ It promotes the development of interpersonal skills, as individuals strive to get on with each other in spite of their differences
- ✔ It promotes mutual understanding of different values, aspirations and cultures (sometimes people are not trying to be difficult, they just have a different mind-set)
- ✔ It promotes social change and progress, as society changes and develops and a culture unfolds
- ✔ It promotes growth as the process of resolution overcomes the stagnation of the status quo (necessity is the mother of invention and conflict is one of necessity's prodigies)
- ✔ It can promote originality and reflection when your viewpoint is challenged

ADVERSE COSTS OF CONFLICT

✖ Higher stress amongst the parties

✖ Lower productivity as effort and resources are redirected into the conflict and away from the work in hand

✖ Lower interpersonal cohesion as individuals - and their supporters - take sides and begin to stereotype each other

✖ Time spent in resolution is taken away from other, more important matters

✖ Inappropriate decisions are made to support the various causes and positions of the parties

✖ Status and ego become more important than reason and reality

✖ The possibility of increased costs to cover negotiation preparation, negotiation time, mediation and/or arbitration costs and, perhaps, legal costs

9

THE FOUR POSSIBLE CONFLICT OUTCOMES

There are four possible outcomes from a conflict situation; only one produces a satisfactory result.

This relates to a branch of mathematics called *game theory* where the outcome and the result can be measured as follows:

Positive sum	**+ 2**	= Party A (+1) and Party B (+1) satisfied and conflict is resolved
Zero sum	**0**	= Party A is satisfied (+1) but Party B is resentful (-1)
Zero sum	**0**	= Party A is resentful (-1) but Party B is satisfied (+1)
Negative sum – 2		= Party A is dissatisfied (-1) and so is Party B (-1) and conflict continues

THE FOUR POSSIBLE CONFLICT OUTCOMES

These outcomes can be drawn as follows:

	I win	I lose
You win	(+2) Positive sum	(0) Zero sum
You lose	(0) Zero sum	(-2) Negative sum

In conflict resolution you work towards the positive sum where both sides are satisfied. In popular language, this is called a *win/win* which, obviously, is the best outcome for all concerned.

TYPES OF CONFLICT

Interpersonal
Ideological clashes - chauvinism v feminism
Dispositional clashes - dominant v mild
Cultural clashes - Arabs v Jews
Religious clashes - Catholics v Protestants
Age clashes - youth v maturity
Value clashes - conservative v liberal

Team/Technical
Sales and Production
H.R. and Fiscal
Research and Operations

National
Wealth clashes - poor v rich
Civil wars

Organisational
Unions and Management
Intra- and inter-company rivalry
Executive competition for resources and top positions

International
The Cold War
War against terrorism

The establishment of a *win/win* is particularly important when the parties are going to be, or have to be, in a long-term or ongoing relationship. Where the outcome is a zero sum or, even worse, a negative sum, the conflict is likely to get worse.

ADDITIONAL CAUSES OF INTERPERSONAL CONFLICT

Conflict between individuals can also be brought about by:

Poor communication
Where the parties are unable to express themselves, verbalise their needs, state the case adequately, provide logical and structured argument, or listen effectively, conflict can arise. The more limited the communication skills a person has, the greater possibility of physical violence.

Perceived differences
Humans form groups naturally and so individuals need to distinguish their group from outsiders. This can lead to possible conflict between races, religions, political systems and, even, teams or departments at work.

ADDITIONAL CAUSES OF INTERPERSONAL CONFLICT

Biological orientation
This stems from the Darwinian concept of the survival of the fittest. Here it is suggested that conflict is both natural and healthy. Nature is *red in tooth and claw*. In the end the strongest survive and those aspects which facilitate their survival are perpetuated. Weak organisations go to the wall.

Spatial relationships
Individuals seem to need their own space. Consequently, when there is overcrowding conflict usually increases.

WAYS OF RESOLVING CONFLICT

WAYS OF RESOLVING CONFLICT

THREE STRATEGIES

Exercise of power
Here, the party with the most power usually wins. Might is right. This is a *win/lose* orientation and the conflict remains because the *loser* still experiences resentment. This competitive approach uses games and tactics to disadvantage the competition and comes from an *I am right and you are wrong* life position. If both parties are fairly equal in power, they could bring about a *lose/lose* catastrophe where no one gains.

Exercise of rights
Decisions fall under the requirements of the law or the prevailing culture for the disputants. Agreements and resolution can be achieved, but this in no way guarantees conflict resolution. In fact, after a decision all those involved can still be dissatisfied (see page 75 on arbitration).

Exercise of mutual interests
Because there is mutual interdependency and the parties usually have to continue living and working together, agreements achieved by recognising mutual long-term interests can bring about solutions that are, for the most part, satisfactory to all concerned. Both parties gain something, a sign of true conflict resolution since all parties continue to work together effectively once the conflict has been resolved.

STYLES OF CONFLICT RESOLUTION

Each of us has a preferred style for resolving conflict, influenced by our personality and experience of dealing with conflict. However, not all conflict situations are the same. If, therefore, we limit ourselves to just one method of resolution we are likely to encounter difficulties where that style is inappropriate.

There are five basic styles that revolve around two axes: the degree of **power** and the degree of **involvement**. All have their advantages and disadvantages.

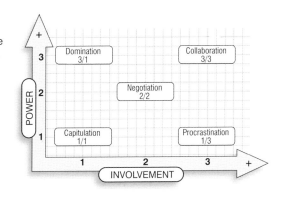

STYLES OF CONFLICT RESOLUTION

Domination (Power 3: Involvement 1)

Where one party is significantly more powerful and does not need the other.

- **Advantage** - You do not have to negotiate if there is no need to do so. For example, management are unlikely to accept a union recognition claim when the union has minimal membership in the plant.

- **Disadvantage** - What goes around comes around. If you take advantage of people when you have power, do not expect any leeway when the situation is reversed. The conflict remains; the aggrieved party is just biding its time for retribution.

Capitulation (Power 1: Involvement 1)

When a party gives in rather than pushing for what it wants.

- **Advantage** - Ideal if you don't need what the other party wants, or you don't have the resources to assist your claim and/or the time is not right.
  He who fights and runs away lives to fight another day.

- **Disadvantage** - Encourages the other side to take more of what they need and sets a precedent and an expectation, should there be future conflict.

STYLES OF CONFLICT RESOLUTION

Negotiation (Power 2: Involvement 2)

Negotiation usually occurs when both parties are dependent upon each other, have the power to frustrate each other and have different objectives. For example, management and unions need each other, and both groups can frustrate each other (lock out/strike). One party has responsibilities primarily to the shareholders, the other to the employees.

- **Advantage** - Though the parties have different agendas, negotiation brings about an agreed sharing of resources. Negotiation reduces the risk of a prize victory to either side, but when done well can achieve a *win/win* outcome.

- **Disadvantage** - Negotiation tends to work from a power orientation as both sides attempt to exert pressure on each other, which is not always conducive to harmony and long-term relations. It can also be costly in time and effort.

(19)

STYLES OF CONFLICT RESOLUTION

Procrastination (Power 1: Involvement 3)

The parties attempt to avoid the situation, hoping that it will go away.

- **Advantage** - Occasionally, the conflict between parties is untimely or incidental and consequently best left unresolved. Like capitulation, the time, your readiness or the situation may suggest that now is not the best time to confront an issue.

- **Disadvantage** - Issues need to be dealt with and the longer they are left the worse they become. *A stitch in time saves nine.*

Collaboration (Power 3: Involvement 3)

Here the parties work together, concentrating on options and outcomes that meet each other's needs and aspirations.

- **Advantage** - In our opinion this is the best form of conflict resolution and will lead to a *win/win* outcome. When achieved there is no residual conflict left suppurating only to become manifest later.

- **Disadvantage** - Collaboration is not always possible. If there is no goodwill, integrity and/or mutual respect from all parties it is unlikely to succeed. Nor does it work when the parties have totally opposing objectives or views.

LEVELS OF CONFLICT

Conflict has a way of growing and it takes on a life of its own as it escalates.
This diagram makes it obvious that the earlier conflict can be resolved,
the better it is for all concerned.

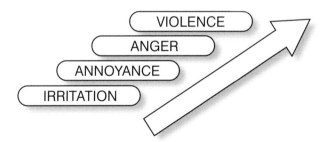

LEVELS OF CONFLICT

Irritation   The problems or difficulties are not significant; you could do without them but they are easily ignored.

Annoyance   The problems bring a growing frustration, stress begins to increase and difficulties are expected. Objections are usually voiced logically.

Anger   The problems bring about strong feelings of injustice, hurt and enmity. Objections start being voiced emotionally.

Violence   The position taken is thought to be totally justified. Retribution and pay-back become the order of the day; there is a need to win, irrespective of the cost, and for the other party to lose. Physical action is thought to be appropriate. Objections are expressed physically because argument using words has been to no avail - people walk off the job, go on strike, abuse the product, etc.

CONFLICT AND PSYCHOLOGICAL DIFFICULTIES

COPING STRATEGIES

Conflict for most people is not enjoyable and a sensible response would be to ensure that it does not arise or it is avoided. Because conflict is inevitable, people sometimes engage in inappropriate psychological defence mechanisms as they attempt to cope with the situation. Coping strategies can include:

Denial
Rather than face an ugly situation, an individual can pretend that it does not exist. Reality is denied, the situation and any discussion about the conflict situation are avoided.

Repression
When denial becomes so extreme that someone is unable to recall the conflict, this is repression. For example, an individual can have strong negative emotions about a person or a group, without knowing why he/she feels so strongly because the original cause is emotionally too difficult to confront again.

COPING STRATEGIES

Projection

Rather than accept the conflict situation and take any responsibility for it, it is projected onto someone, or something, else. Thus, an innocent bystander in a situation could be forced into the role of victim.

Displacement

When power differences make it impossible or inappropriate to be angry with a person or group, or there is a social or other constraint, then the anger is referred onto another, usually weaker, party. For example, an employee may be taken to task by his manager, the employee in turn is bad tempered with his wife, so the wife snaps at their son, who kicks the cat - this is displacement.

Intellectualisation

Here the conflict is spoken about in a clinical and abstract way with no recognition of individual emotion or involvement. Conflict usually generates a lot of emotion, and if this is ignored then total resolution is not normally achieved.

CONFLICT AND PSYCHOLOGICAL DIFFICULTIES

COPING STRATEGIES

Regression
Sometimes, because the conflict is difficult to
manage, an individual may regress to
behaviours that he or she successfully used
as a child in order to cope with stress
and/or pressure. Such behaviour could
include crying, stamping feet, shouting
or refusing to speak.

Fantasy
Rather than deal with the real world in
which there is conflict, the individual
breaks away into prolonged fantasy. In
extreme cases an individual may report
things that were said - believing them to
be true - when, in fact, they are a fantasised
version of events.

COPING STRATEGIES

Minimization
Conflict difficulties are discounted so that they are spoken about as insignificant and not worth discussion or acting upon. By trivialising the conflict, the individual is protected in the short-term from the unpleasantness of dealing with or confronting the situation.

Fixation
The individual holds on to a particular aspect of the conflict and will not move forward, thus avoiding bringing up other aspects of the conflict which would be more difficult to manage. In this way they fixate on one element and prevent any progress towards resolution.

CONFLICT AND DISTORTED THINKING

Sometimes people are drawn into conflict situations because their thinking is distorted. Towards the end of the arguing stage conflict resolution becomes difficult, because the thinking processes and the logic being employed by the parties begin to break down as emotions and ego start to dominate.

Once you recognise distorted thinking in yourself or in the other protagonists, it can be managed so that resolution is achieved more quickly.

CONFLICT AND DISTORTED THINKING

Here and on the following two pages are the more common forms of distorted thinking.

Pejoratives and over-generalisations

One incident becomes *always* or *never*, thus a general conclusion is based on just one piece of evidence. For example:

You *never* help when………	*All* shop stewards are…………..
Every manager is……………..	Management *always*……….
You *always* ignore our claims	*Everybody* knows that…………

- It is better to provide specific examples of behaviour

Shoulds

The application of absolute rules of black and white, right and wrong, good and bad when in reality there are many variations in between. Those adopting this approach usually have very strong views on most things, especially the behaviour of others. Their favourite words include *should, ought* and *must*. Some people just *should* all over the place!

- It is more helpful to think in terms of grey; life has many beautiful colours besides black and white

CONFLICT AND DISTORTED THINKING

Catastrophising (doomsdaying)
This is about making one small incident into a total disaster - in common parlance, *making a mountain out of a molehill*.

Eg: 'If you don't give us a 10% pay rise many of our people will not be able to pay their rent and will starve.'

Or: 'If we gave a 10% pay increase, it would cripple our commercial viability and bring an end to this company and also the local community.'

- It is far better to keep as much as possible in perspective

Personalisation
When someone takes everything as an attack on them personally. Situational conflict is brought down to an individual level.

Eg: 'When he talks about poor team performance he is really talking about me.'
'He has always had it in for me because he dislikes me.'

- It is more constructive to take oneself out of the equation

CONFLICT AND DISTORTED THINKING

External control

The view here is that nothing can be done because everything is in the lap of the gods or in the hands of lady luck. Everyone involved in the conflict is a victim of fate. There is no point in trying to improve the situation because you cannot win whatever you do.

- It is much better to take control where you can and take personal responsibility for those things that you can change

Internal control

This is the opposite of external control: people feel that what they say will happen. They have an exaggerated belief in their own powers.

- A realistic view of one's power and influence makes discussion easier

Being perfect

Here individuals cannot face being wrong in any way. They automatically assume that they are correct and everyone else is wrong. *Sorry* is not in their vocabulary.

- We all need to accept our own inadequacies and vulnerability

CONFLICT AND PSYCHOLOGICAL DIFFICULTIES

CONFLICT: A SIMPLE MODEL

THE AGREEMENT BOX

Conflict usually occurs when two (or more) parties have difficulty with each other. This causes *tension* which increases immediately or over time, forcing the parties to confront each other. The conflict is then either resolved, or a stalemate occurs or the conflict continues.

A way of thinking about and reducing conflict is to find what is called *the agreement box*. In conflict there are two extreme positions taken over what is possible or available:

Usually, the position taken is an ideal between *what I would really like* and *what I will accept*. So it works like this:

CONFLICT: A SIMPLE MODEL
THE AGREEMENT BOX (Cont'd)

When the positions overlap we have *the agreement box*:

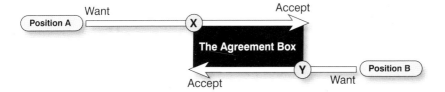

Any agreements between the two positions x and y, that is anywhere in the agreement box, will be acceptable to both parties.

The trick is to get the other side to move towards your position faster than you move towards theirs. Get them to run to you whilst you walk to them!

CONFLICT: A SIMPLE MODEL

THE AGREEMENT BOX (Cont'd)

To be successful it helps to know:

- Not only what the other person (or side) wants, but what they will settle for
- What you and they are willing to give up or trade/bargain so that you can move towards the agreement box
- What you will expect in return if you are going to bargain

When the other person trades more than you do, the closer resolution will be to what you want.

Any resolution in the agreement box usually achieves a *win*/*win* solution because both sides settle within their agreement limits.

GAMES AND CONFLICT RESOLUTION

FOUR TYPES OF GAMES

Essentially, games are ways of exerting pressure on the other stakeholders in order to persuade them to give way or make concessions. Games are not always helpful. When you recognise a particular game is being played, it can be put into perspective and managed. Sometimes these games are called gambits or tactics.

A helpful way of classifying games is as follows:

- **Opening games**   to establish dominance or procedures in your favour
- **Advantage games**   to assist and strengthen your position
- **Disadvantage games**   to weaken your opponent's case
- **Closing games**   to speed a conclusion in your favour

GAMES AND CONFLICT RESOLUTION

FOUR TYPES OF GAMES

Essentially, games are ways of exerting pressure on the other stakeholders in order to persuade them to give way or make concessions. Games are not always helpful. When recognise a particular game is being played, it can be put into perspective and aged. Sometimes these games are called gambits or tactics.

way of classifying games is as follows:

ng games   to establish dominance or procedures in your favour

e games   to assist and strengthen your position

e games   to weaken your opponent's case

s   to speed a conclusion in your favour

CONFLICT: A SIMPLE MODEL
THE AGREEMENT BOX (Cont'd)

When the positions overlap we have *the agreement box*:

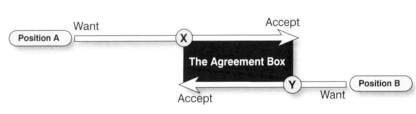

Any agreements between the two positions x and y, that is anywhere in the agreement box, will be acceptable to both parties.

The trick is to get the other side to move towards your position faster than you move towards theirs. Get them to run to you whilst you walk to them!

CONFLICT: A SIMPLE MODEL

THE AGREEMENT BOX (Cont'd)

To be successful it helps to know:

- Not only what the other person (or side) wants, but what they will settle for
- What you and they are willing to give up or trade/bargain so that you can move towards the agreement box
- What you will expect in return if you are going to bargain

When the other person trades more than you do, the closer resolution will be to what you want.

Any resolution in the agreement box usually achieves a *win/win* solution because both sides settle within their agreement limits.

GAMES A
RESOL

GAMES AND CONFLICT RESOLUTION

OPENING GAMES

I only deal with decision-makers
Purpose: to intimidate or to ensure they are working with the right person.

That is not negotiable or is *off limits*
Purpose: to attempt taking something off the agenda that they do not want. In fact, everything is always negotiable.

The mandate
Purpose: to set out their most favoured position - 'Corporate cannot afford and will not support any claim in excess of 5%'.

This is the agenda
Purpose: to get the other side to follow your agenda rather than one that is agreed.

ADVANTAGE GAMES

Nothing but the facts

Purpose: to show that their case has hard evidence to support it and that, consequently, it is realistic, reasonable and fair, and should be accepted without question.

Ask for the moon

Purpose: to overstate what they want so much that they can trade down considerably without coming to a real settlement position, eg: asking for 15% when they would settle for 5%. When you are pushed back to 10% they can put on an honest face and say, 'Look, we have conceded 33% already'.

ADVANTAGE GAMES

Comic
Purpose: to use humour to divide the other person's position, eg: 'You want what?! You can't be serious; even my mother-in-law would not try that. I did not get off the boat yesterday you know!'.

The link
Purpose: once they have identified something you want, and they can concede with little cost, then they link it with something that they want and treat the two as one item, eg: 'We can increase the rate by 2% if you forgo an increase in sick pay and a reduction in hours'.

DISADVANTAGE GAMES

Testing
Purpose: to make you doubt your strength, eg: 'You know your management could not take a transport strike on a public holiday' or 'I'm confident that your members would not strike over this issue'.

Russian Front
Purpose: to offer something that you want, together with a totally unacceptable alternative, eg: 'Do you want to do this or go to the Russian Front?' 'We can offer you 3% this year or nothing this year if you agree to 10% next year'.

See you in court
Purpose: to intimidate you. They end the discussion saying, 'See you on the picket line' or 'See you in court/tribunal'.

Abuse
Purpose: to offside you by rudeness, attacking your credibility, status, making you wait, taking interruptions, etc.

CLOSING GAMES

All or nothing
Purpose: to force a close, eg: 'If you do not accept this then we go back to square one and start again'.

Time limit
Purpose: to accelerate the conclusion, eg: 'This offer finishes today' or 'Prices go up tomorrow' or 'The boss comes back tomorrow and he would not approve this'.

Bonus
Purpose: to encourage settlement through giving something small, eg: 'If we settle today then we will....'.

DEALING WITH GAMES

The best defence against a game is to point out to the player that you recognise the game for what it is, eg. 'Because that is such an inappropriate alternative, you know that playing the Russian Front gambit is really not helping this negotiation'.

Another approach is to play a game called *Broken Record* (from *The Assertiveness Pocketbook*) and ignore the person's game or gambit and just repeat yourself over and over again. If you do this often enough game players soon stop playing their games.

Sometimes it is appropriate to challenge the person with a question - eg: 'Why do you find it necessary to shout/abuse/question my authority?' - said in a manner of genuine inquiry.

It is important not to take offence or to get emotional when games are played. Games are not personal, they just go with the territory of conflict resolution. In fact, spotting them, and their variations, can be fun.

NEGOTIATION

PRINCIPLED NEGOTIATION

Principled negotiation has a very different approach from that of *the agreement box* (explained earlier). It is an interesting way of resolving difficulties, developed by Fisher and Ury.

Principled negotiation suggests that it is the agreement between the parties that counts and is important because it is founded on the mutual respect the parties have for one another.

When the parties can agree on the principles in a situation, or on what is fair and what is right, then agreements come quickly and a *win/win* solution becomes possible.

PRINCIPLED NEGOTIATION

These are the steps suggested by Fisher and Ury:

Step 1: Don't take a position. To do so only leads to argument and causes difficulties with the other side, who will be forced to take a counter-position in response to yours.

Step 2: Separate the people from the problem. This prevents you attacking the opposition and holding them responsible for the situation. This minimises difficulties caused by ego and status. It also helps to reduce emotions and mutual blame.

Step 3: Focus on interests. This moves the argument away from positions and towards solutions. By asking *why?* you can understand what is really wanted. In this way you can put the problem before your preferred solution, and you can continue to be hard on the problem but soft on the people involved.

BATNA

The best alternative to a negotiated agreement (BATNA for short) was developed, once again, by Ury and Fisher in order to help assess an offer. A BATNA helps to measure a proposal against a realistic alternative. With a BATNA you review what would happen if you did not get an agreement.

Basically, the better your alternatives to what is being offered, the stronger your position. Conversely, the fewer attractive alternative options you have, the less power you have.

A PROCESS FOR BATNAS

Step 1: If you fail to agree, list all the options available to you. Take the best options and make them as realistic as possible. Work out what you have to do to make your short list possible.

Step 2: Put as many of your options as possible into effect.

Step 3: Assess all or any offers that you have. If they are an improvement on your BATNA then accept; if not, try and improve the offer and if this fails then fall back on your BATNA.

Continued over page…

A PROCESS FOR BATNAS (Cont'd)

Step 4: Invent options for mutual gain. Here the more possible solutions you have the better, as this strategy broadens opportunities for both sides. Look for mutual gain and dovetail differing interests.

Step 5: Insist on objective criteria. Going for external standards avoids both ego and position stances. Take the view that you only want to do that which is right. Each difficulty is framed as an agreed search for objective criteria. In this way you do not yield to pressure but only to principle.

This section is based on: *Getting to Yes* by Fisher, Ury and Patton; and *Getting Past No* by Ury. Both books published by Random House Business Books.

PERSONALITY TYPES
AND CONFLICT

PERSONALITY TYPES AND CONFLICT

MYERS BRIGGS

The way normal people prefer to approach things reveals their personalities, their differences and their preferences. People differ in the way they prefer to:

- Obtain their energy to get themselves going
- See and perceive things in the world
- Make decisions
- Manage and organise their lives and their work

Such differences can bring about misunderstanding, resulting in frustration with the other person who has a different preference. If misunderstood, this can lead to conflict.

Although there are many exceptions, when two individuals are in conflict - and it is not over the allocation/use of a resource - then it probably results from differences in personality type. Remember, no one personality type is better than another. We are all as individual as our fingerprints or our DNA. Just as we can choose to use our non-dominant hand, so we can choose to behave using a different preference. After all, preferences are just that - preferences.

*This section is derived from the work of Katherine-Briggs and her daughter Isabel Myers Briggs who interpreted the work of C.G. Jung in developing the MBTI®, currently the most popular instrument for assessing the personality of an individual.

EXTROVERTS, INTROVERTS AND CONFLICT

Extroverts are energised by the outside world, whereas introverts much prefer to go into themselves to be energised. Thus, extroverts will find out what they think and what they believe by talking, discussing and arguing with others.

Introverts, on the other hand, tend to find it much easier to reflect, think and review things quietly on their own.

Extroverts talk first and this helps them to think. Introverts think first and this helps them to talk.

Conflict might occur when a) an extrovert cannot understand why an introvert will not talk to him/her about a conflict problem and b) an introvert cannot understand why an extrovert won't think through the situation first before talking and arguing.

PERSONALITY TYPES AND CONFLICT

SENSORS, INTUITIVES AND CONFLICT

People can have two very different ways of experiencing the world.

Sensors like to employ all of their five senses to gain facts and details about things that are going on in the present. When they talk they are literal, specific and usually detailed. Decisions are made when the facts and the figures are there to support a chosen option.

Intuitives are naturally drawn towards the big picture and the patterns, possibilities and options, as well as the meanings and connections between things. In discussions with others, concepts and ideas are more readily available than facts and figures. Decisions tend to be made based on possibilities which rely on implications that are there to support them.

Conflict can occur when the sensors want to stay with the facts and the detail, while the intuitives want to concentrate on the implications of the big picture. When looking at a problem, neither individual *sees* the same thing.

THINKERS, FEELERS AND CONFLICT

Thinkers like to base conclusions on facts using logic and analysis, and like to achieve objective truth as far as possible. Thus, they find it easy to separate themselves from a situation and be dispassionate in their approach.

Feelers are comfortable about making decisions according to their personal values, and usually strive for harmony and well-being. Feelers place importance on emotions and empathy for the individuals involved in the situation. This, for them, is more important than the facts of the situation. Whilst they can recognise the significance of logic and objective content, they prefer not to use them if disharmony and bad feeling are likely to be the outcome.

This is not about how clever individuals are, it is about differences in preferred processes in coming to a decision or a conclusion. In conflict situations thinkers will seek the most logical solution, whereas feelers strive for the most harmonious outcome. What is logical and what is harmonious are not usually the same.

Thinkers try to persuade by logic and feel frustrated when feelers are influenced by emotions. Feelers want to decide from the heart; thinkers are ruled by the head.

JUDGERS, PERCEIVERS AND CONFLICT

This is about how people like to organise their lives. Judgers are usually organised, structured, like to make plans and start working on things early so that deadlines can be comfortably met. They like to make decisions and work with minimum diversions. Judgers love closure.

Perceivers find it easy to collect information before coming to a conclusion. In their approach to life they are more free and easy, adaptable and flexible. They prefer spontaneity rather than structure, and tend to dislike deadlines. Perceivers need to *feel* a deadline before they will work towards it. They are more at ease when they do not need to have a schedule and would rather not be orderly in their work. Perceivers like to keep things open.

Conflict can arise when judgers want closure on a situation and work to create a structure to achieve it and then move on. They come into difficulty when perceivers attempt to keep the situation fluid by keeping their options open for as long as possible.

MEN AND WOMEN AND CONFLICT

Men and women differ psychologically in some respects. To explain this it is necessary to fall back on pejoratives and gross generalisations, if not down-right sweeping stereotyping with all its exceptions. Even so, most people would agree that:

Women like to talk about problems
Men prefer just to offer solutions

Men hear facts and sometimes miss the emotional content
Women listen to the emotional content and sometimes miss facts

Women like to take time over a decision
Men like to decide quickly

Men like to hide their emotions
Women like to show their feelings

Women like to multi-task
Men like to do things one at a time

Men are more interested in things than people
Women are more interested in people than things

There are thousands of exceptions to what is suggested here, but many of the above have been the basis of conflict between men and women since Eve persuaded Adam to eat the apple - or did Adam want to eat it in the first place? If you are having difficulty with someone of the other sex, reflect on the above to improve mutual understanding.

INDIVIDUAL NEEDS AND CONFLICT

Ignoring people's basic behavioural needs/processes can cause problems. The examples below are obvious but often overlooked as sources of conflict by management/employees.

- When faced with change, people usually say *no* before they say *maybe* before they say *yes*; the harder the change, the longer the *no* period
- Individuals do things they think are sensible - for their reasons, not yours
- If you attack someone's logic you offend their ego
- Individuals will work towards goals if they have helped set them
- Forced compliance only changes behaviour, not the heart or mind
- If you use your formal authority to get a response, it will be just that - formal
- Individuals are motivated by self-interest and respond better to being asked, not told
- Positive rewards bring more lasting compliance/change than do threats of punishment
- To influence an individual start from where they are, not where you are
- In changed behaviour there is always a tendency to slip back to the old ways
- Most people prefer to remember only the good things in the past
- People can only accept information that is within their own frame of reference
- Perception alters reality with respect to what people want to see, hear or believe

A FORMULA FOR PREVENTING CONFLICT

For very minor issues and disagreements, application of the following formula can often reduce potential conflict and bring about a discussion rather than a full blown argument. It does not work all the time, but is very useful nevertheless.

The process is:

Affirmative statement	You agree with the person
Softening statement	You show that you understand their position
Flag	You indicate that you have something to say
Give reasons for your position	You help them understand your position
Negative statement	You say 'no'
Offer a compromise if appropriate	You offer an alternative where you can

You can see that it works rather like judo - you walk alongside the person before you turn them. If you just said 'no' the tension would rise with the likelihood of conflict developing. Even if you just said 'no because…', you still might get an argument. By responding in judo fashion, you appear reasonable and, if there is to be an argument, it begins with facts rather than emotions (referred to elsewhere).

A FORMULA FOR PREVENTING CONFLICT

EXAMPLE

The manager's request:	'I want you to come in and work this Saturday morning.'
The employee's response:	
Affirmative	'Yes.'
Softening	'We have been exceptionally busy; everyone has been very rushed recently and there is a backlog. I can see why you need me.'
Flag	'But I have to tell you…'
Reason for refusal	'…the difficulty is that this Saturday my son is playing in his soccer final and I just must support him.'
The refusal	'So I am sorry, I just cannot come in this Saturday.'
Compromise	'If it is of any help, I could stay behind on Thursday and Friday?'

A FORMULA FOR PREVENTING CONFLICT

EXAMPLE

The employee's request:	'Can I have next Thursday morning off to have my dental check-up?'
The manager's response:	
Affirmative	'Yes.'
Softening	'It is very important to look after your teeth and regular check-ups are essential.'
Flag	'But I have to tell you...'
Reason for refusal	'...that this week as you know is month-end and we must get all the reporting done by Friday.'
The refusal	'So I need you on Thursday.'
Compromise	'See if you can change the appointment to next week.'

PERSONALITY TYPES AND CONFLICT

SOCIOGRAMS

Sociograms are useful for identifying sources of potential interpersonal conflict in teams and for creating teams of people who will work together well.

It is a fact of life that we find some people more attractive than others. We enjoy their company and their conversation. For others the synergy is just not there. There may also be differences in culture, power, status, aspiration, education and a host of other things that bring about different levels of liking or understanding between people.

At a basic level the sociogram maps out who relates well to whom.

PERSONALITY TYPES AND CONFLICT

SOCIOGRAMS

For instance, in a group of five people we could have:

David likes John and James
Jennifer likes John and Mary
James likes David and John
John likes James and Mary
Mary likes John and James

If you drew this as a sociogram it would look like this:

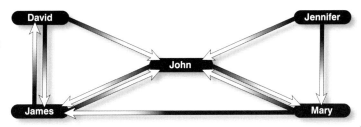

PERSONALITY TYPES AND CONFLICT

SOCIOGRAMS

From the sociogram on the previous page you can see that:

- John could work with almost anybody
- David, James and John would make a good team
- John, James and Mary would work well together
- You would have to be careful about Jennifer, who is nobody's first choice, but she would like to work with John and Mary
- If David and James were put with Jennifer there could be interpersonal conflict
- If you put Mary and David together sparks might fly

Sociograms are also useful for working out aspirations and positions of stakeholders, as well as for anticipating alliances.

They will also tell you who is likely to be bullied (see final chapter on harassment and bullying).

CONFLICT
RESOLUTION PROCESS

THE FOUR STAGES

Just as there are many causes of conflict so too are there many approaches to its resolution. However, most conflict is resolved through a process which by and large looks like this:

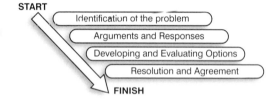

START

Identification of the problem

Arguments and Responses

Developing and Evaluating Options

Resolution and Agreement

FINISH

Not all conflict resolution follows this outline, nor are all the stages necessary for a satisfactory outcome, but the model does represent the generic process. There are no magic processes or formulas to conflict resolution, but the above process will help by alerting you to what stage is coming next and what you should be working towards.

Sometimes parties get stuck in conflict. It then becomes more important to achieve movement in the process rather than concentrate on the specific issues of difficulty or differences.

CONFLICT RESOLUTION PROCESS

THE FOUR STAGES

Identification of the problem
This can be in neutral or emotional/argumentative statements, eg: 'Given the accepted interest rate, your price is totally unacceptable' or 'You greedy devil, do you think I got off the boat yesterday? Your price is ridiculous'. In both of the statements the problem has been identified, namely: *the price charged is thought to be too high for the purchase*.

The first statement, being based on facts, is much easier for someone to work with than the second which is emotionally charged.

To begin well it is best to discover the facts - and stick to them - and keep the discussion anchored on the problem you want to resolve.

Do not work with opinions, hearsay or emotions. They are important but peripheral to the problem itself and are open to denial. Facts are less able to be disputed.

THE FOUR STAGES

Arguments and Responses

This is the *toing and froing*, during which those involved put their case as strongly as possible - usually employing games (see page 36) and distorted thinking (see page 28) to support their respective positions.

Since neither side can force the other side to comply completely with their wishes or aspirations, this stormy beginning is followed by the generation of possible options.

Work with the other person, discover where they are coming from and why they have taken the position they have. You do not have to agree with it, but to achieve movement you need to work from it.

THE FOUR STAGES

Developing and Evaluating Options

In this stage ideas are generated, solutions suggested, concessions made and bargains struck. Depending on power, needs, timing and the conflict context, a possible option gradually becomes acceptable to both sides. As it is an improvement on the BATNA (see page 46) it is accepted by both sides.

Resolution and Agreement

Here the stakeholders agree on an option or line of action which hopefully, for the most part, is acceptable to both sides and felt to be fair. In an ideal situation it is a *win/win* outcome.

Resolution could be formal, as in a joint statement, or less formal as in a handshake or verbal agreement. Whatever form of agreement, *those involved accept that the conflict is resolved*.

67

CONFLICT RESOLUTION PROCESS

LEARNING

The wise person, having come through and resolved a conflict situation, would do well to reflect on the process and content, in order to learn from what happened. Do this by asking questions such as:

- What went well?
- What helped?
- What hindered?
- Are relationships better or worse?
- What did I learn?
- What will I do differently next time?
- How might the situation be improved next time?

By reflecting on what you have learned, you maximize on your experience and develop your skills in conflict resolution.

CONFLICT AND THIRD PARTY INTERVENTIONS

MEDIATION AND ARBITRATION

Obviously, it is best if those in conflict can resolve matters themselves. Sometimes, those involved, whether individuals, groups or even nation states, are so far apart - because of emotions, history, status, power differentials, etc - that they need help to find a resolution.

Third party intervention can be arranged by those concerned, or it can result from a prior contractual agreement. Alternatively, it may be imposed by law. There are two types:

1. Mediation: the mediator helps both parties to understand the various positions of the stakeholders, in the hope that a mutually acceptable agreement is possible.

2. Arbitration: usually the stakeholders make representations to the arbitrator, who then presents a solution which is binding on all parties.

Some forms of conflict suit mediation, others suit arbitration. It's difficult to arbitrate when emotions or relationships are involved, while mediation is not that useful when there are legal or contractual obligations. Broadly speaking, people with problems enjoy mediation and corporate bodies go to arbitration. But there are always exceptions.

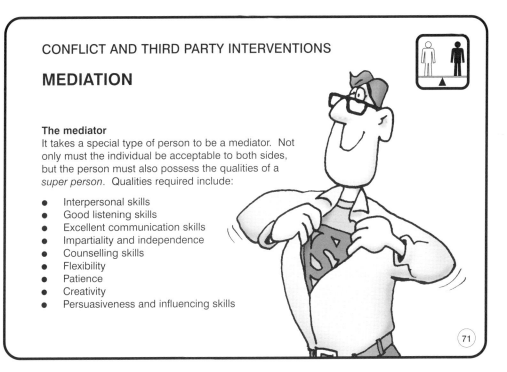

CONFLICT AND THIRD PARTY INTERVENTIONS

MEDIATION

The mediator
It takes a special type of person to be a mediator. Not only must the individual be acceptable to both sides, but the person must also possess the qualities of a *super person*. Qualities required include:

- Interpersonal skills
- Good listening skills
- Excellent communication skills
- Impartiality and independence
- Counselling skills
- Flexibility
- Patience
- Creativity
- Persuasiveness and influencing skills

MEDIATION

The mediator

A good mediator must also have maturity, experience and knowledge of the process of mediation, and high personal ethical standards. The mediator's main role is to help the parties explore each other's position and needs, and to keep them focused on - and working towards - a resolution. The mediator must be infinitely involved with the issues and committed to the participants, while at the same time remaining independent and non-judgemental. This difficult balancing task has to be achieved while at the same time moving the process toward a conclusion that is satisfactory and welcomed by all concerned.

Problems with intervention abound. Does the mediator give advice or remain on the sidelines? Does he/she act as an advocate on behalf of one party to another? If there is an obvious difficulty or pitfall looming, does the mediator raise it with the parties or let them discover it for themselves? Should there be an intervention during arguments, and what if arguments result in violence?

THE MEDIATION PROCESS

There are four basic steps in the mediation process:
1. **Open**
2. **Discover**
3. **Unite**
4. **Close**

1. Open

Opening begins the mediation.
The mediator's role and the way the mediator would like to move forward in the process of resolution are set out.

The *rules of engagement* are agreed, along with how the parties will relate to each other and how there should be mutual respect and an absence of blame.

73

THE MEDIATION PROCESS (Cont'd)

2. Discover
The needs of each party, their aspirations and concerns are presented; misperceptions are clarified. Every effort is made to help the parties understand their own positions and those of the other stakeholders.

3. Unite
Once both sides have outlined their positions, options for solutions can be encouraged, generated and evaluated. Possible concessions and bargains can be suggested and reviewed. Tentative agreements and bargains can be struck and time frames can be agreed.

4. Close
This captures the mutual agreements, ensuring that all parties are satisfied and that the resolution is acceptable, pragmatic and perceived as fair. Sometimes a review process is built into the agreement. Agreements can be set down on paper or accepted verbally.

ARBITRATION

Here an independent third party decides on the final outcome, which is legally or contractually binding on both sides. The parties go to arbitration knowing they have to abide by the final decision, even if they disagree with it.

Consequently, the arbitrator (unlike the mediator) is directly interested in the content, facts and reasons that resulted in conflict, because he/she must weigh all the evidence, arguments and surrounding factors before coming to a decision. There has to be a judgment which the arbitrator feels reflects the facts and is fair to all.

Arbitration is particularly useful when there is conflict over facts, a point of law or a contractual detail that can only be resolved by an expert's ruling. Thus, arbitration is usually employed in commercial situations. It offers little when the substance of the dispute is more emotional than objective. If the parties want justice or vindication, arbitration is not seen as satisfactory.

Arbitration also suits protracted conflict, when there is stalemate between the parties. This is because arbitration, unlike mediation, does not require co-operation between those in conflict. This is why, in some cases, once mediation has failed, arbitration is a viable alternative.

ADVANTAGES OF ARBITRATION

- ✔ Both sides can put their case openly
- ✔ It does not need the goodwill or trust of the parties to move the process forward
- ✔ It does not require process skills to move the debate forward
- ✔ It allows for expert evidence to be heard
- ✔ The process is objective
- ✔ The process is open to third party inspection
- ✔ It can balance unequal power distribution between the parties
- ✔ The parties can use advocates if they feel inadequate or are not used to presenting their case or complex issues for themselves
- ✔ It can work to a fixed timetable
- ✔ The outcome can be binding in law on the parties

DISADVANTAGES OF ARBITRATION

- ✖ It can be costly, which would disadvantage the financially challenged
- ✖ It does not take account of the emotional needs of the parties
- ✖ It encourages an adversarial approach, with each party taking the strongest and, consequently, the most extreme position they can; in addition, it calls for excellent verbal and presentation skills
- ✖ The process is fixed and allows for very little variation
- ✖ It may end in a lawful settlement which might not be a just settlement
- ✖ It may settle the difficulties between the parties but the conflict, especially the emotional component, can remain
- ✖ It is possible for an outcome to be imposed that is thought to be unacceptable to those involved, and so the conflict is far from being resolved

CONFLICT AND THIRD PARTY INTERVENTIONS

THE MANAGER AS MEDIATOR

Frequently, managers have staff who, for various reasons, don't get on. This can have an adverse effect on efficiency and productivity. Mediation will help, but also note:

- There are always at least two sides to every conflict
- People need their *shout* before they can consider another viewpoint
- Sometimes people prefer to wallow in the problem rather than be part of the solution
- Protagonists find it difficult to provide information that is not in their favour
- The first side you hear usually sounds the most plausible
- Protagonists think their position is the most logical/appropriate
- Individuals expect you to take their side in every argument
- Once people take a position their egos get involved
- Most people find it difficult to admit they're wrong or to say *sorry*
- In conflict, some protagonists can be more interested in getting even than getting a fair resolution
- Having taken a position, it's difficult for protagonists to appreciate a viewpoint different from theirs for reasons of ego
- Sometimes it benefits the protagonists to maintain the conflict rather than solve it

CONFLICT AND THIRD PARTY INTERVENTIONS

SOME MANAGEMENT TACTICS

- Remain neutral at all times
- Work on the outcome, not on who is right or wrong or allocating blame
- Separate facts from emotions
- Separate history from hearsay
- Separate the people from the problems
- Test positions for credibility
- Suspend judgement for as long as possible
- Help the two sides respect each other
- Test what is acceptable to both sides
- Estimate what is the best and worst outcome for both sides
- Work out what it would cost for a protagonist to change their position
- Consider whether a change in viewpoint would cost the person in terms of loss of *face* or humiliation

CONFLICT AND THIRD PARTY INTERVENTIONS

A POSSIBLE MANAGEMENT PROCESS

- See each party individually and in private, and take extensive notes
- Reflect on what the real issues are, how the situation has arisen and what is really important to the parties and why
- See each party again to clarify any issues arising, resolving matters of fact and using this period to help the parties gain respect for each other
- Reflect on possible outcomes and options that might be appropriate and that the parties would accept
- See both parties individually; leading with your reasons, state what you think might be reasonable in the circumstances, stressing the superordinate needs of the organisation over and above those of the individuals concerned
- See both parties together, representing one to the other and presenting the outcome that you would like - working towards an agreement that is acceptable to both sides

TEAM CONFLICT

TEAM CONFLICT

WAYS TO OVERCOME

Conflict within a team can arise for the same reasons as inter-departmental conflict: resource allocation, role ambiguity, interdependence and, additionally, personality differences (see page 50).

Ways of overcoming conflict could include:

- Agreeing a very clear operational statement as to what is expected of the team - making and discussing decisions in the light of that statement, thus reducing individualism and people's personal needs

- Wherever possible, ensuring that the team contains no more than seven people (it is difficult to relate psychologically to more than seven people at any one time, and sub-teams develop bringing associated conflict of *in groups* and *out groups*)

TEAM CONFLICT

WAYS TO OVERCOME

- Hold regular *safe* team meetings, where process issues and differences, as well as operational issues, are reviewed
- Provide opportunities for the team to interact socially as well as operationally, and ensure every effort is made to recognise and celebrate the team's successes
- Ensure that team members understand each other's preferred team roles and how - because of their different personalities and contributions - they can best contribute to the team in their preferred role which is different from their functional role (see here the work of Belbin)
- Support, encourage and reward mutual respect for all individuals within the team

CONFLICT OVER DISCIPLINE

This refers to *misconduct*, not *gross misconduct*. With gross misconduct, the employee leaves the organisation and the conflict between individual and employer is brought to an abrupt end. Misconduct usually concerns poor performance or unacceptable behaviour on the part of the employee, which does not warrant dismissal in the first instance.

Suggestions for reducing conflict arising out of discipline include:

- On appointment, tell the employee what is and is not acceptable performance, behaviour and attendance (confirm this in writing)
- Tell new employees how the disciplinary process works and what rights and prerogatives they have
- See the employee as soon as possible after alleged misconduct
- Advise the employee what he/she has done that is to be challenged, giving enough time for the person to prepare an explanation
- Remind the employee that they were told when appointed what was unacceptable behaviour
- Present evidence concerning the employee's misconduct in a factual way

CONFLICT OVER DISCIPLINE

Suggestions for reducing conflict arising out of discipline (cont'd):

- Give the employee and/or a representative of their choice the opportunity to state the reasons for their alleged behaviour and any extenuating circumstances
- Ensure the employee's case is heard by someone who was not directly affected by the behaviour or conduct of the employee at the time
- Carefully consider the employee's explanation and investigate any facts that are different or new
- If necessary and appropriate, seek the views of witnesses
- Give due consideration to the employee's explanation and make a decision as to whether there was poor performance/misconduct or not
- Consider the length of service of the employee - the longer the service, the more appropriate a degree of leniency
- Where discipline is considered appropriate, decide what is reasonable in the circumstances, communicate the decision - what it will be and the reasons for it - to the employee and their representative, and confirm this in writing together with how the employee can appeal
- Tell the employee what will happen if the unacceptable behaviour is repeated

CONFLICT OVER DISCIPLINE

If necessary, training should be given to the employee to help him or her improve.

- Should the employee disagree with the decision or think it unfair or unreasonable in any way, then he or she should be encouraged to appeal to a more senior manager who has not previously been involved, and who has the authority to reverse the initial decision if necessary

- If discipline is recorded then the misdemeanour should only remain on the person's file for a set predetermined time before it is taken off or *spent*

- Each misdemeanour should exist in and follow its own procedure, ie: it would be unfair to discipline someone for, say, absenteeism, then for poor workmanship, then insubordination and then they are dismissed - they should all run conterminously with warnings for each type of misconduct

CONFLICT AND THE ORGANISATION

Frequently, conflict within organisations is brought about by different requirements and practices for budget allocation, resources, performance and deadlines. These can be between levels of management and/or between operational functions and the service departments that support them.

Difficulties can occur when there are changes in the market, technology, procedures, policy and people. Rules and different expectations can also create conflict.

If this is not enough, there is also interpersonal conflict that arises when people just do not like each other and find it difficult to get on.

So, summarising we have:

- **Management conflict**   policy, budgets, direction
- **Functional conflict**   procedures, resources
- **Role conflict**   performance, methods
- **Interpersonal conflict**   people

CONFLICT AND THE ORGANISATION

Whilst conflict in organisations is inevitable, there are some basic principles that will help to reduce potential difficulties:

Clear mission and vision statements
When decisions are made in line with the agreed mission and vision, they are depersonalised. One department is not favoured over another. Instead, allocations are made in the light of the agreed direction of the organisation.

Clear values
These set norms of behaviour. Whether you are a chairperson or a tea person, everyone is accountable and judged by the same values.

Open communications
Difficult to achieve without time and effort. Emphasis should be placed in two ways, interpersonal communication including MBWA (managing by walking about) and an active open door policy - which is no good if no one walks through it!

Be ethical
Have integrity in all your dealings. Treat your superiors, colleagues and employees with the same respect and deference as you would your customers.

CONFLICT AND THE ORGANISATION

Dealing with organised labour
Here are some principles adopted by firms who seem to have fewer industrial relations problems than others:

- Pay at the 75% percentile for the greater part of the pay period. It is much better than the average, yet allows those who are money hungry to go elsewhere. There is nothing worse than having disgruntled employees who, because of the golden handcuffs, cannot afford to go elsewhere. Your reputation for being a *good payer* will attract better candidates who will, in turn, make the firm more profitable.

- Follow the marketplace conditions of employment and give a condition that you are going to have to give anyway before it is requested. If you are going to have to concede it, why make the employees negotiate for it? Such a strategy only teaches employees that to achieve improvements they must generate conflict.

CONFLICT AND THE ORGANISATION

Dealing with organised labour (cont'd)
- Follow agreed procedures since they are binding on all parties. If you have procedures for discipline, appeals, arbitration, etc then follow them.
- Follow both the letter and the spirit of the legislation regarding labour law, health and safety and code of conducts. Sharp practice, even if it is legal, will lead to conflict.

Precedent
Keep to precedents. What you do for one you will be expected to do for all. What management do today, they will be expected to do tomorrow unless there is very good reason for change. Managers are notorious for getting a quick solution today at the expense of conflict in the future, because of the precedents that are created.

Standards
Apply the same rules for all. There is something inequitable about management golf days and a tough absenteeism policy for employees.

Promises
These are to be kept. If you make an agreement, don't make employees or the trade union police it.

Bullying and Harassment

BULLYING AND HARASSMENT

DEFINITIONS

Bullying is the tendency for one employee to oppress, harass or
intimidate another - either verbally, physically or emotionally or all
three - within the work environment. It includes unwarranted
criticism, excessive fault finding, over-monitoring and, even,
unjustified warnings.

Here is a Trade Union definition:

'Persistent, offensive, abusive, intimidating or insulting
behaviour, abuse of power or unfair penal sanction which
make the recipient feel upset, threatened, humiliated or
vulnerable which undermines their self-confidence and
which may cause them to suffer stress.'

MSF Union 1994

Note: excellent information on bullying and the inspiration for
this section came from Tim Field's useful website:

 www.bullyonline.org

BULLYING AND HARASSMENT

THE STATISTICS

According to research at UMIST on 70 organisations and 5,500 employees:

10.5% had been bullied in the last six months
24.4% had been bullied in the last five years

According to a Staffordshire University Business School study:

53% of employees had been bullied during their careers to date

According to research at UMIST and Goldsmiths College, covering 5,288 adults:

11.4% of males had been bullied in the last six months
 9.9% of females had been bullied in the last six months
22.0% of males had been bullied in the last five years
27.7% of females had been bullied in the last five years

Similar percentages are found by researches in the USA and Australia.

These figures show that bullying is a real source of conflict at work and requires serious attention by management.

TYPICAL BULLY BEHAVIOUR

There is usually a fixed and predictable pattern to a bully's behaviour. It varies only in consequence of the bully's tendency to be both opportunistic and predatory. Here are some examples of bullying behaviour, but the list is only illustrative and by no means exhaustive:

- Making unreasonable demands for work output or performance
- Causing humiliation in the presence of others
- Undertaking exceptionally close and unnecessary supervision of work
- Denying access to resources that the employee needs to achieve KPIs
- Isolation, at work and/or socially
- Treating people unfairly or differently compared with others, in terms of work load, remuneration, benefits, etc
- Ignoring views of others, overruling decisions, ridiculing decisions, denying legitimate requests and belittling contributions
- Swearing, using abusive language and name-calling when there are no witnesses
- Making threatening telephone calls
- Using aggressive e-mails or memos with threats of discipline
- Downgrading job titles and positions

BULLYING AND HARASSMENT

WHY BULLYING IS SO DIFFICULT TO MANAGE

- Bullying for greater output/performance can be couched in and presented as good management, giving legitimate 'stretch' to employees

- Departments with high production usually get left alone because senior management's attention is usually directed to problem areas or low productivity: in these situations a bully who makes staff work excessive hours is likely to escape notice, and when complaints are initially made, the first response is often one of incredulity

- The bully is usually the immediate manager of the victim, and the difficulty is that it is only through this person that a grievance procedure can be initiated

- The bully usually *pre-conditions* those concerned - the HR Department and other centres of power and influence within the organisation - regarding the fact that he/she has a *problem child* in the department and that he/she is working on it

WHY BULLYING IS SO DIFFICULT TO MANAGE (Cont'd)

- Bullying usually begins with a slow insidious build-up of small acts of intimidation, which makes a complaint difficult because single actions look trivial

- It is difficult to get evidence because of the opportunistic nature of bullying, done without witnesses and thus difficult to substantiate

- Where someone is bullied publicly, colleagues are either too intimidated to object or defend the individual, or they think, *rather them than me*

- Many firms do not have a policy which deals with bullying, nor do they list bullying as gross misconduct, punishable by instant dismissal

BULLYING AND HARASSMENT

HELP FOR THE BULLIED

The company's perspective

- Have and enforce a company policy on bullying, stating a zero tolerance for such behaviour and the disciplinary implications

- Make harassment and bullying a matter for gross misconduct and state that employees who bully will be dismissed for just one offence

- Set up an employee hotline, so that an aggrieved employee can bypass the usual grievance procedure in situations where the bully or harasser is the immediate manager of the victim

- At induction of new employees, set out what they can reasonably expect in the way that they will be managed and what they should do if these expectations are not met

- Train HR on the topic of bullying, including how to recognise potential and actual bullying behaviour as well as how to manage victims

- Ask HR to monitor and explore sudden adverse changes in absenteeism or turnover levels

HELP FOR THE BULLIED

A colleague's perspective

- Do not be a silent bystander when you see a colleague being bullied
- Provide solace and support to a colleague victim
- Actively encourage an employee to use the grievance procedure for redress for each and every bullying situation
- Be prepared to sign *round robins* of complaints to report a bully
- Be a *whistle blower* on bullying
- Support the victims as they go through the grievance procedure
- Be prepared to act as a witness or a representative/advocate for your colleague(s)
- Keep a written record of the bully's negative acts, evidence that can be used when the bully denies his or her actions
- Suggest to HR that there should be a policy on bullying if one does not already exist

BULLYING AND HARASSMENT

HELP FOR THE BULLIED

The victim's perspective

- Develop assertiveness skills (see *The Assertiveness Pocketbook*) and use them as soon as you realise that you are being bullied, especially those skills which enable you to:

  - express your feelings
  - express your rights
  - use 'I' statements

  - say 'no' to unfair or inappropriate demands
  - keep control of your emotions and keep to facts and behaviours

- Make a list of all your achievements inside and outside work from as early as you can remember and read your list regularly to yourself; this will help you preserve your ego, strength and self-confidence (no one can take away from you what you have achieved in the past, and the best indicator of future performance is past performance); this negative situation will not last

- Keep a log of every bullying event including what was said, when it was said and the way it was said; write up every instance as soon as possible afterwards; do not keep this log at work; look for patterns that will help you anticipate the bully's behaviour and provide evidence for your HR Department

HELP FOR THE BULLIED

The victim's perspective (cont'd)

- Get support from your colleagues at work and significant others in your life
- Inform your union or staff representative
- Read everything you can on bullying
- Read the company policy on bullying; leave the policy prominently on your desk; check for precedents and for what the company has done in the past in cases of bullying
- Go direct to your manager's manager if you are being bullied by your boss; keep notes of all discussions and meetings
- Use the company's grievance procedure, again keeping a full note of all your actions
- If all else fails and neither your company nor your colleagues support you, leave the company if you can, but not before you have another job to go to; then claim constructive dismissal against your old employer through the Tribunal system

BULLYING AND HARASSMENT

IS IT BULLYING OR IS IT HARASSMENT?

Bullying	Harassment
Usually begins slowly before you realise it is happening	You know immediately that you have been harassed
Is usually based around competency issues	Usually to do with sexuality and/or gender
Is about control and domination	Is about ownership and possession
Brings about feelings of inferiority and self-doubt	Brings about feelings of fear
The affronts are psychological	The affronts are sexual
Takes place at work	Begins at work and tips over to social life
Never just one incident	Can be a single incident

DEFINITIONS OF SEXUAL HARASSMENT

Sexual harassment can take many forms and may include:

- Deliberate and unsolicited physical contact or unnecessary close physical proximity
- Repeated sexually orientated comments or gestures about a person's gender, body, appearance or life-style
- Offensive phone calls, letters or e-mail messages
- Stalking
- Showing or displaying sexually explicit graphics, pictures, cartoons, photographs or internet images
- Questions or insinuations about a person's private life/relationships/friends
- Persistent invitations to social activities after the person has made it clear they are not welcome
- Sexually explicit jokes and propositions

International Labour Office 2001

'Sexual harassment: where any form of unwanted verbal, non-verbal or physical conduct of a sexual nature occurs with the purpose or effect of violating the dignity of a person, in particular when creating an intimidating, hostile, degrading, humiliating or offensive environment.'
The European Commission

BULLYING AND HARASSMENT

THE STATISTICS

As reported in research commissioned by The European Foundation for the Improvement of Living and Working Conditions, not only is the incidence of sexual harassment high, but in certain sectors of the UK economy it is rife:

54% in a national study
47% reported in a study by an employment agency
89% in the health service
90% in the police force

Costs
In an EOC study of 54 cases, successful applicants received awards of between $750 to $40,000 with the majority of cases being settled at between $2,000 and $5,000.

These costs do not include lost management time, preparation time and the costs of legal advice and representation fees. Loss of goodwill through adverse publicity is also significant.

FIVE MYTHS ABOUT SEXUAL HARASSMENT AT WORK

Myth 1: **Harassment policies now make the reporting easy.**
Fact: Very few people who experience harassment file formal complaints.
In an EOC study 48% of applicants left their jobs before they applied to a Tribunal for redress.

Myth 2: **Harassment is a rare occurrence.**
Fact: Harassment is reported by about 40-60% of women and 10-20% of men.

Myth 3: **Harassment stories are either lies or fabrications.**
Fact: The EOC study of 54 tribunal cases found that 34 (63%) were successful.

Myth 4: **Harassment is brought about by the way women dress or behave.**
Fact: Women are harassed irrespective of age, appearance, behaviour or dress.

Myth 5: **Harassment is either trivial or done in fun.**
Fact: The EOC study showed that in 90% of the cases the applicant had lost their job or resigned as a result of sexual harassment.

BULLYING AND HARASSMENT

WHAT IS HARASSMENT?

This covers a whole host of unacceptable behaviours, including:

- The words people use, the tone they use and how they say things
- Throwaway comments
- Sexual or stereotyping jokes
- Sexual or stereotyping pictures, cartoons, verse - on paper, walls, boards, faxes or computers
- Any type of touching
- Standing too close
- Downloading or circulating offensive material
- Gestures or mimicking that could be interpreted as sexual, sexist, racist, anti-gay, disablist, etc
- Sexual behaviour of any sort
- Isolating or segregating others
- Humiliating initiation rites

OBLIGATIONS FOR EMPLOYERS

Your employer/manager:

- Must not harass you
- Must not let you harass anyone else at work
- Must not let anyone else at work harass you
- Must not let anyone you come into contact with through your work harass you - even if they are not employed by your company

BULLYING AND HARASSMENT

HARASSMENT QUIZ

	Yes	No	Maybe
1. If you touch someone is it harassment?			
2. Does an employee have to object before it counts as harassment?			
3. Is asking a fellow employee out on a date harassment?			
4. If I use words like 'darling', 'love', 'wog' in a friendly way, can I be accused of harassment?			
5. Is it only employees who can be disciplined for harassment?			
6. If I don't invite someone to social activities at work, can it be counted as harassment?			
7. If someone suddenly complains about the way I have always behaved, can it be counted as harassment?			
8. If what I say is not deliberate or I don't intend it to be insulting, can that be taken as harassment?			
9. If, on my own personal computer, I download pornographic or racist material from the internet is that harassment?			
10. If it is part of the culture to tell gay, racist, sexual or sexist jokes, can I do the same?			

ANSWERS TO THE HARASSMENT QUIZ

1. **Yes**. If you touch people in certain places it is bound to be harassment. Also, if you touch them in a sexual way it is harassment. The degree of touching is culturally based: apparently, Italians touch one another more than most other European nations, and Britains are the least *touchy*. However, some people have an aversion to being touched whatever their nationality, so it is best not to.

2. **No they don't**. They might feel too embarrassed to ask you not to, or not have the assertiveness skills to say anything - especially if you are their manager or someone in authority. In body language, senior people demonstrate their seniority by touching more junior staff. Play safe and do not touch another employee.

3. **Yes**. You can ask once but if the other party says 'no' that is it. Further requests - even with flowers - count as harassment.

4. **Maybe**. You have to be absolutely sure that the person you are with does not mind.

5. **No**. Anyone who comes into contact with a person at work cannot harass that person. It is up to the employer to protect all employees in all aspects of their work.

ANSWERS TO THE HARASSMENT QUIZ

6. **Maybe**. This is a difficult one. You can have lunch on a regular basis with your friends but if someone is left out of all social activities that occur at work, an employer might have difficulty proving the individual was not being harassed.

7. **Yes**. Your most recent action could be counted as the last straw, effectively pushing the complainant over the edge and causing him/her to object. If you continue then that is harassment.

8. **Yes**. You can have no intention of harassing an individual, but what constitutes unacceptable behaviour lies with the person who feels harassed and not with you. Harassment is in the ear of the hearer.

9. **Maybe**. If someone else saw it, or if you or a group of you looked at it in the presence of someone who objected, then that is harassment.

10. **Maybe**. It is difficult to know who you might offend. Some people can tell a joke and no offence is taken; you tell the same joke and it causes offence. It is best not to tell jokes that might cause offence.

WAYS OF REDUCING HARASSMENT CONFLICT AT WORK

- Develop an anti-harassment policy and a procedure for complaints - 72% of *The Times* top 100 firms have an anti-harassment policy in place

- Make relationship training available for all staff, especially during induction

- In appropriate training events cover the skills of giving and receiving feedback about behaviour at work - these skills are useful in appraisal, disciplinary sessions and for individuals to self-police in cases of unacceptable behaviour

- Act immediately on any complaints and treat them seriously and with sensitivity

- Deal with the complaint through the grievance procedure and move to discipline if the matter is well-founded, irrespective of who is involved

- Provide a help-line if employees are likely to find the grievance procedure inoperable: an EOC study showed that in 33% of the cases the harasser was the director or the owner, and in 66% of the cases it was the employee's immediate line manager

- Publish and communicate results to show that harassment is not acceptable

- Work hard on developing an organisational culture, in which every individual is treated with dignity and respect

About the Authors

Max A. Eggert BSc, MA, FCIPD, CFAHRI, ABPS, MAPS
Max is a management psychologist specialising in assisting individuals reach their maximum potential. Besides being retained by major international corporations as coach, mentor and strategist, he has been interviewed frequently on TV, radio and in the print media both in Australia and in Europe. Max has degrees in psychology, industrial relations and theology. He has fifteen books in print in twelve languages, one of which is a standard text and two are frequently in the ten best business books. Several of his books are on the recommended reading lists of Sydney, London, Harvard, Westminster and Sussex Universities.

Contact: Transcareer Pty Ltd. Level 31, 88 Phillip Street, Sydney, NSW 2000.
Tel: +61 2 8211 0500   Fax: +61 2 8211 0555   Mobile: 040 360 2286
E mail: max@transcareer.com.au

Wendy Falzon
Wendy is an HR professional working in the areas of interpersonal development and maximisation of talent for both individuals and organisations. Her expertise includes career development, coaching, conflict resolution and team integration. Wendy is married, lives in rural New South Wales, is an accomplished singer and has a consuming passion for tennis.

First published in 2004 by **Management Pocketbooks Ltd**.
Reprinted 2005, 2007. All rights reserved.

© Max A Eggert and Wendy Falzon, 2004.

British Library Cataloguing-in-Publication Data – A catalogue record for this book is available from the British Library.

Design, typesetting and graphics by **efex ltd**.

Printed in U.K.

ISBN 978 1 903776 06 3

ORDER FORM

Your details
6.99

Please send me:

	No. copies
The Resolving Conflict _____ Pocketbook	[ ]
The _____ Pocketbook	[ ]
The _____ Pocketbook	[ ]
The _____ Pocketbook	[ ]
The _____ Pocketbook	[ ]

Name _____

Position _____

Company _____

Address _____

_____

_____

Telephone _____

Fax _____

E-mail _____

VAT No. (EC companies) _____

Your Order Ref _____

Order by Post
MANAGEMENT POCKETBOOKS LTD
LAUREL HOUSE, STATION APPROACH,
ALRESFORD, HAMPSHIRE SO24 9JH UK
Order by Phone, Fax or Internet
Telephone: +44 (0)1962 735573
Facsimile: +44 (0)1962 733637
E-mail: sales@pocketbook.co.uk
Web: www.pocketbook.co.uk

MANAGEMENT POCKETBOOKS

Handwritten annotations:
M1082816 09/10/07
048678 658 4095
EGG
6.99
✓